NE WiDE RiVER To CROSS

NE WIDE RIVER TO CROSS

Adapted by BARBARA EMBERLEY   Illustrated by ED EMBERLEY

Little, Brown and Company   Boston • Toronto • London

ISBN 0-316-23445-1

Library of Congress Cataloging-in-Publication
information is available.

10 9 8 7 6 5 4 3 2 1

WOR

Published simultaneously in Canada
by Little, Brown & Company (Canada) Limited

Printed in the United States of America

Old Noah built himself an ark,

He built it out of hick'ry bark.

The animals came in one by one,

And Japheth played the big bass drum.

The animals came in two by two,

The alligator lost his shoe.

The animals came in three by three,

The ostrich and the chickadee.

The animals came in four by four,

The hippopotamus blocked the door.

The animals came in five by five,

The yak in slippers did arrive.

The animals came in six by six,

The elephants were doing tricks.

The animals came in seven by seven,

A drop of rain dropped out of heaven.

The animals came in eight by eight,

Some came in by roller skate.

The animals came in nine by nine,

The cats and kittens kept in line.

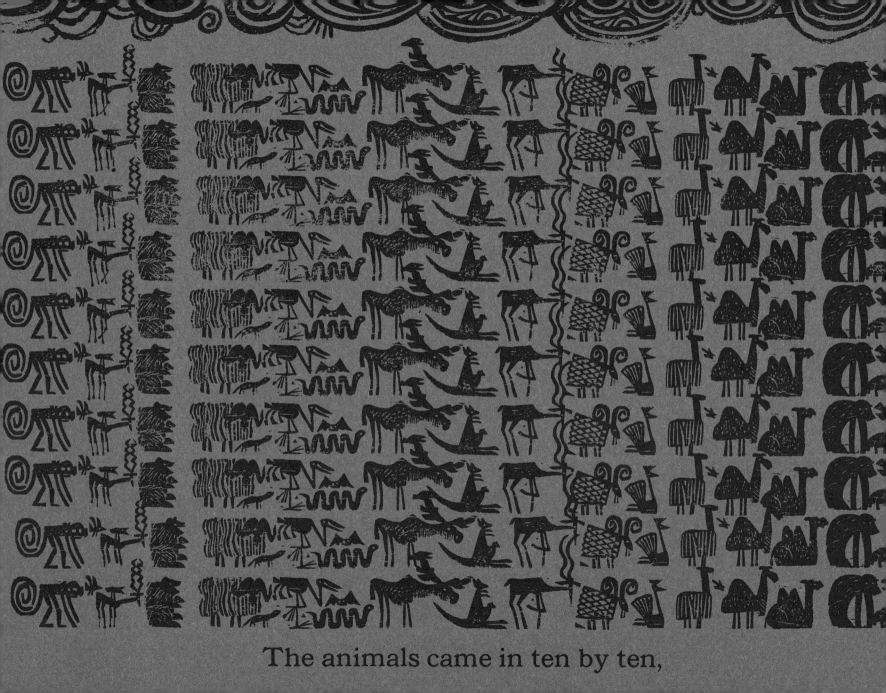

The animals came in ten by ten,

Let's go back and start again.

One wide river, and that wide river is Jordan,

One wide river, there's one wide river to cross.

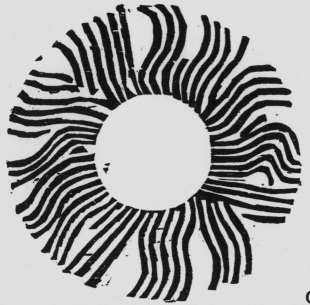

It rained and rained and
rained till the high hills and all
the mountains were covered.
The waters receded and the ark
came to rest on the mountains
of Ararat. To show that He
would never again send such a
flood, God set a rainbow in the sky.

ONE WIDE RIVER TO CROSS

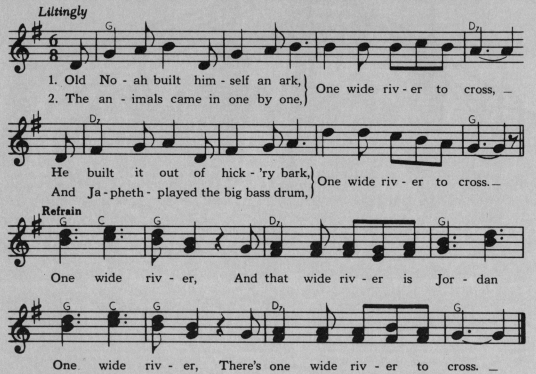

Liltingly

1. Old No - ah built him - self an ark,
2. The an - imals came in one by one,
One wide riv - er to cross, —

He built it out of hick - 'ry bark,
And Ja - pheth - played the big bass drum,
One wide riv - er to cross. —

Refrain

One wide riv - er, And that wide riv - er is Jor - dan

One wide riv - er, There's one wide riv - er to cross. —